STUFF UNICORNS LOVE

JESSIE OLESON MOORE

Adams Media

New York London Toronto Sydney New Delhi

Adams Media
An Imprint of Simon & Schuster, Inc.
57 Littlefield Street
Avon, Massachusetts 02322

First Adams Media hardcover edition DECEMBER 2017

ADAMS MEDIA and colophon are trademarks of Simon and Schuster.

For information about special discounts for bulk purchases, please contact Simon & Schuster Special Sales at 1-866-506-1949 or business@simonandschuster.com.

The Simon & Schuster Speakers Bureau can bring authors to your live event. For more information or to book an event contact the Simon & Schuster Speakers Bureau at 1-866-248-3049 or visit our website at www.simonspeakers.com.

Interior design by Sylvia McArdle
Interior illustrations by Jessie Oleson Moore

Manufactured in the United States of America

10 9 8 7 6 5 4 3 2 1

Library of Congress Cataloging-in-Publication Data
Moore, Jessie Oleson, author.
Stuff unicorns love / Jessie Oleson Moore.
Avon, Massachusetts: Adams Media, 2017.
LCCN 2017035849 | ISBN 9781507205693 (hc) | ISBN 9781507205709 (ebook)
LCSH: Unicorns--Humor. | BISAC: HUMOR / Topic / Animals. | SOCIAL SCIENCE / Folklore & Mythology.
LCC PN6231.U54 M66 2017 | DDC 818/.602--dc23
LC record available at https://lccn.loc.gov/2017035849

ISBN 978-1-5072-0569-3
ISBN 978-1-5072-0570-9 (ebook)

Always follow safety and commonsense cooking protocols while using kitchen utensils, operating ovens and stoves, and handling uncooked food. If children are assisting in the preparation of any recipe, they should always be supervised by an adult.

DEDICATION

To my very own blessing of unicorns, Olive and Porkchop.
I love younicorn.

CONTENTS

5

ACKNOWLEDGMENTS

There's no freaking way I could have written this book without a little help from my friends. First and foremost, I'd like to thank Sprinkle the unicorn for being an able, magical, and creative coauthor. I'd also like to thank all of the other unicorns consulted during the process of writing this book.

Cotton candy—coated gratitude goes out to Eileen Mullan and Brendan O'Neill at Adams Media for believing in A) unicorns and B) this project.

A glittering shooting star of gratitude to Alexandra Penfold, my agent, longtime supporter, and Official Unicorn Consultant.

Tender loving cuddles to Porkchop and Olive for being my constant loves, companions, and supporters during the writing of this book.

Magical rainbow sparkle bubble kisses go out to Team Unicorn, who helped advise with suggestions, unicorn puns, and overall support, including, but not limited to: Margie Moore, Jenna Graham, Rebecca Patt, Natalie Fox, Kasey Brooks, and (OMG) the loyal followers of my website, CakeSpy.com—and its associated social media pages—who I suspect are indeed the best-ever resources for crowdsourcing on unicorn-related subjects.

INTRODUCTION

Welcome to *Stuff Unicorns Love*! This book was written by unicorns for humans, and is a giant, sugar-coated celebration of all the things that unicorns love the most.

Inside these pages you'll discover what makes unicorns tick and what tickles their fancy. From rainbows and cotton candy to dance parties and sprinkle-covered donuts, unicorns really know how to have fun and live it up. Now, for the first time ever, they want to share their favorite things with us humans.

#unicorns

Unicorns are highly misunderstood creatures, so as you read this book, here are a few things you should keep in mind:

- Unicorns speak a magical language that is almost impossible for humans to understand.

- Unicorns are pretty shy creatures. They tend to dodge the spotlight as much as possible, which is why you probably never see them around!

- Unicorns don't have hands. While their hooves are fantastic for galloping and are sufficient for holding cupcakes or cotton candy, they are not as well suited to writing or typing with expediency.

Because of all these reasons, the unicorns needed a human (ahem... me!) to help translate all their secret true feelings into what they call "people language." With the help of my trusty unicorn BFF, Sprinkle, I created a book that embodies the mystical and slightly mischievous unicorn spirit. So get ready for cotton candy clouds, glitter-covered-hoof high fives, and an intense amount of rainbow-colored magic. On behalf of unicorns everywhere, enjoy!

GET TO KNOW SPRINKLE!

Meet my unicorn BFF, Sprinkle!
Sprinkle was born in Cotton
Candy Canyon and studied
Human-ities at Unicorniversity.
He—yes, Sprinkle is a he—
loves the smell of cotton candy,
eats uni-cornflakes for breakfast
every morning, says his favorite
vegetable is carrot cake, and
loved every minute of helping me
write this book. Say hi, Sprinkle!

Part 1

GET TO KNOW UNICORNS

You probably already know a few basic facts about unicorns: they have horns, they love rainbows, and they are extremely magical. But there's so much more to learn! In this section you'll get the lowdown on all things unicorn, from where they live and what they love to who they date and even how they poop. Yum!

UNICORN CODE: THE 3 RULES EVERY UNICORN MUST FOLLOW

The first step to understanding unicorns is thinking like a unicorn.
To do that, follow the three main pillars of unicorn life:

1. Always be ready to find delight in anything at any time.
There's so much mystical, rainbow-colored fun to be had in
the world that shouldn't be missed!

2. If you are feeling blue, eat a pound of candy and then dance around
to '80s music for at least twenty minutes. Repeat steps as necessary
until blue feeling has turned to rainbow.

3. You must always, always, *always* believe in magic.

what is a
unicorn
made of?

WHAT IS A UNICORN?

In the human world, unicorns are defined as rare mythical creatures that live in magical mystery. While a unicorn most closely resembles a pony with a horn on its head, unicorns have their own unique DNA.

A unicorn is made up of equal parts magic, sweetness, and love, with a little bit of delight and mischief thrown in. Mix it all together, and poof! You have a mystical unicorn.

WHERE DO UNICORNS LIVE?

Look up at the clouds and the blue sky above you. Even though you can't see it, just beyond there is another level of the sky where the air smells of freshly glazed donuts and the pink clouds are made of cotton candy.

This, my friends, is where unicorns live.

Lucky for us humans, unicorns have the ability to soar down to Earth whenever they want. Not only does this allow them to keep tabs on the human world, but it also allows them to keep up to date on the professional Ping-Pong circuit, which they just can't get enough of!

Unicorns do tend to be secretive, so keep a close eye out. You might be surprised to learn that they're not quite as rare as you think!

WHAT'S THE DIFFERENCE BETWEEN A UNICORN, A PEGASUS, AND A PONY?

Sometimes a unicorn is confused with its magical counterpart, the Pegasus, or its earth twin, the pony. In fact, two of the most common questions unicorns are asked are "Where are your wings?" and "Are you related to ponies?"

While they are all part of the *Mystical Pony* genus, there are some important differences between these creatures that you should know:

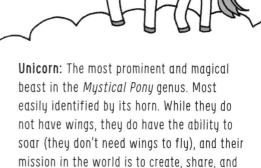

Unicorn: The most prominent and magical beast in the *Mystical Pony* genus. Most easily identified by its horn. While they do not have wings, they do have the ability to soar (they don't need wings to fly), and their mission in the world is to create, share, and spread magic.

Pegasus: Characterized by their flying wings; no horn. Slightly less magical than unicorns.

Pony: Has neither wings nor horn. While the pony does still possess a sweet and loving heart, it doesn't have any special powers.

ALL ABOUT THE HORN

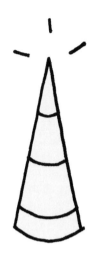

A unicorn's horn is his or her most recognizable feature and is the symbol of the unicorn's magical powers. But in the Unicorniverse, the horn isn't a horn at all—it's called a corn, hence, the uni*corn*.

While some unicorn scholars say that the unicorn's corn comes from the Latin *cornu*, meaning "a structure with a shape likened to a horn," it actually comes from the horn's close resemblance to the magical unicorn food staple known as candy corn.

Unicorns were even originally known as unicandycornhorns, but thankfully, over time, the name has been shortened to unicorns. Phew!

Why do unicorns have horns?

The unicorn's horn developed as a way of holding donuts, one of the unicorn's favorite snack foods. These tasty round treats helped keep the unicorns' tummies full as they went on adventures across rainbow valleys and buttercream cloud forests.

Over time though, unicorns have discovered many other uses for their horns, including:

- Holding rainbow bagels
- Creating art
- Playing ring toss
- Turning off beeping smoke alarms
- Serving as built-in swizzle sticks
- Defending the honor of princesses

Do they have feeling in the horn? They sure do! So please ask before touching, and never try to twist it.

Does the horn really have magical properties?

Legend has it that the unicorn's horn has the ability to neutralize poison. If you ask a unicorn, though, he or she will say the ability to hold donuts remains its most magical property.

UNICORN SENSES

Believe it or not, unicorns experience the favorite basic senses—sight, sound, touch, taste, and smell—much differently than humans do. For instance:

Sight: Everything that unicorns see is a little bit more magical than what humans see. It's slightly sparkly around the edges, and sadness or anger is delicately blurred out.

Sound: Unicorns have something called selective hearing, which means their ears filter out things that aren't sugary sweet to hear. For instance, you might find a unicorn tuning you out when you're talking about the latest juice cleanse or fantasy football. Try bringing up Funfetti cupcakes, '80s music, or classic Trapper Keeper art instead.

Touch: Hugs and cuddles actually provide nutrition to the unicorn soul. If you ever encounter a unicorn, please ask if you can give him a hug. If he says yes, remember to turn your head to the side as you go in for the hug so you don't get a horn to the eye.

Taste: Unicorns are "taste blind" to almost all savory foods, except, of course, for pizza. In the Unicorniverse, pizza is actually considered a health food. For the most part, unicorns survive and thrive on cupcakes, cookies, cotton candy, and other sweets.

Smell: A unicorn's olfactory sense is programmed to pick up pleasant scents and filter out the unpleasant aromas. This means they are quick to detect the scent of honeysuckles, freshly baked cookies, and birthday cake, but they remain blissfully unaware of offensive scents such as stinky feet.

UNICORNS' SIXTH SENSE

Unicorns also possess the sense of magic. What does the sense of magic feel like? Picture the moment you opened your dream Christmas present at age six, or the way you feel the moment before you blow out the birthday candles. Humans get a flicker of this magical sense at times, but for unicorns, it is a constant.

UNICORN SALUTATIONS

How do unicorns say "hi" and "bye" to one another? And how do they express that something is totally awesome or super secret?

Saying hi: Unicorns greet one another by crossing horns and nuzzling muzzles.

Hoof bump: A common greeting for "bronicorns" is to curl their arms and let the outsides of their hoofs bump together.

bRONiCORNS

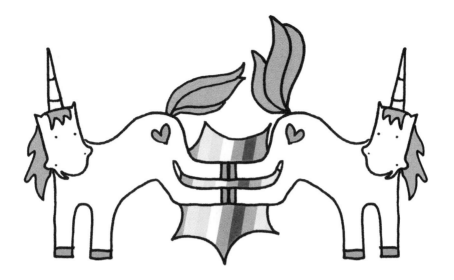

High five: The unicorns' equivalent of a high five looks kind of like a donkey kick, but a rainbow starburst happens when their hooves make contact. Do not try this at home.

giggle

tee Hee

Horn-touch: Unicorns touch horns after telling secrets; it's just like when humans pinky-swear.

Saying bye: Unicorns touch rump-hearts as they part (yes, there's one on either side).

5 FUN FACTS ABOUT UNICORNS (FROM THE HUMAN WORLD)

Unicorns *love* to keep secrets, so it's no wonder we know so little about them. Here are five facts about unicorns that you may not have heard before.

1. A group of unicorns is referred to as a "blessing." Makes sense! After all, we are #*blessed* to even know these magical critters exist.

2. The unicorn is the national animal of Scotland and features prominently in the nation's coat of arms. Just for fun, can you say "unicorn" with a Scottish brogue?

3. There is a unicorn-shaped constellation of stars called Monoceros on the celestial equator. Maybe that's why unicorn eyes sparkle like stardust.

4. Alexander the Great claims to have ridden a unicorn. Yeah right, Alexander—unicorns say they much prefer Uber-ing around.

5. Legend says the throne chair of Denmark, commissioned around the 1660s, is made of unicorn horns. This, of course, is another lie.

5 FASCINATING PIECES OF UNICORN TRIVIA

How much do we *really* know about unicorns?

1. Nine out of ten unicorns agree that bubble gum is the best pizza topping.

2. Cotton candy is by far one of the most important foods in the unicorn world. The average unicorn consumes 88.8 pounds of cotton candy per year.

3. It's true: unicorns fart rainbows.

4. The most popular condiment in the unicorn world is glitter. In fact, jars of the sparkling stuff appear on restaurant tables the same way salt and pepper shakers do in human restaurants.

5. Competitive horn fencing is one of the most popular unicorn sports, followed by ring toss and plate spinning.

#TRUTH

THE SCOOP ON UNICORN POOP (AND MORE)

Recently humans have become obsessed with unicorns' bodily functions—everything from unicorn farts to burps, but most importantly unicorn poop. So is unicorn poop really as sweet as we hoped?

Well, if you are what you eat, then it's no wonder that unicorn poop really is sweet.

Like the creatures who produce it, unicorn poop is made of magic. It often varies in texture, from meringue cookie–like to more soft serve–esque, but nearly always has a rainbow tint and is 100 percent safe for human consumption.

Oh, and in case you were wondering: unicorns sweat rainbow sprinkles, which are also suitable for human consumption, and they burp and fart rainbows, which always smell like freshly baked cookies.

HOW DOUBLE RAINBOWS ARE REALLY MADE

HOW RAINBOW SPRINKLES ARE REALLY MADE

What's the best part of a unicorn dance party? All the sprinkles they make while they work up a sweat dancing away to '80s hits!

THE HISTORY OF UNICORNS

Unicorns have been soaring through sugar clouds and having glitter parties for centuries now. Here are just a few rainbow-letter dates from their unique history:

1962: Shel Silverstein records his song "The Unicorn." In 1968 the song was re-recorded by The Irish Rovers, became a smash hit, and was quickly established as the unofficial theme song for unicorns. (And the piece reached a new audience when it was included as a poem in Silverstein's famous 1974 volume, *Where the Sidewalk Ends*.)

400 B.C.: Unicorns go mainstream! Greek writer Ctesias mentions unicorns for the first time in his book *Indica*.

1871: *Through the Looking-Glass* by Lewis Carroll is published. The book features the tale "The Lion and the Unicorn."

1505 or 1506: Artist Raphael paints the masterpiece *Young Woman with Unicorn*.

1968: The book *The Last U...* by Peter S. Beagle is publis... It is later adapted into an a... mated film (ask any unicorn... the movie was better).

PAINT ME

STOP WAR

Circa A.D. 1224: Genghis Khan has an encounter with a unicorn that convinces him to abandon his plan to attack India. Unicorns are very charming...

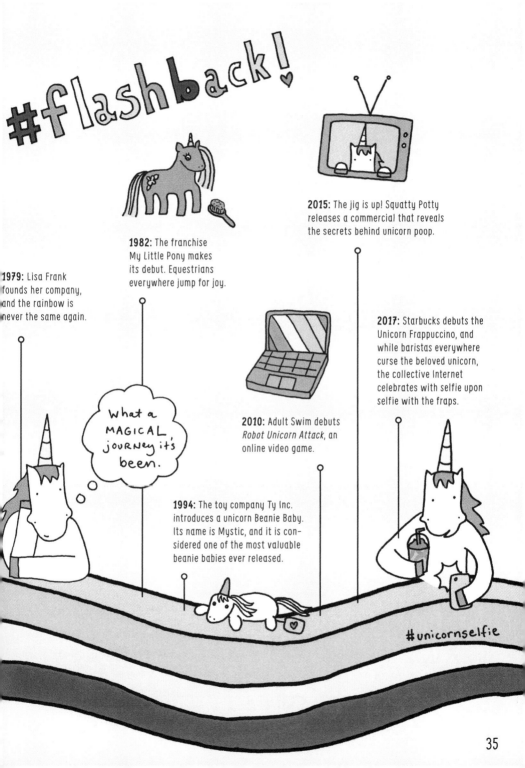

#flashback! ♥

1979: Lisa Frank founds her company, and the rainbow is never the same again.

1982: The franchise My Little Pony makes its debut. Equestrians everywhere jump for joy.

2015: The jig is up! Squatty Potty releases a commercial that reveals the secrets behind unicorn poop.

2017: Starbucks debuts the Unicorn Frappuccino, and while baristas everywhere curse the beloved unicorn, the collective Internet celebrates with selfie upon selfie with the fraps.

What a MAGICAL journey it's been.

2010: Adult Swim debuts *Robot Unicorn Attack*, an online video game.

1994: The toy company Ty Inc. introduces a unicorn Beanie Baby. Its name is Mystic, and it is considered one of the most valuable beanie babies ever released.

#unicornselfie

GROWING UP UNICORN

When a baby unicorn is born, it's called a babycorn. Its horn is little more than just a nub, or as unicorns lovingly call it, a "corn niblet." The babycorn is, indeed, as cute as you might imagine.

As a babycorn grows, its horn becomes more prominent. As a kiddicorn, the young unicorn will enter school, where he or she will be exposed to a number of different mystical subjects, including Magic, Delight, Whimsy, and Happiness.

As the unicorn becomes older, it is considered first a uni-tween and then a uni-teen. While the uni-tween is awkward and giggles a lot, the uni-teen tends to be world-weary and surly. Don't worry; it's only temporary!

TOP BABYCORN NAMES

These names are some of the most popular babycorn names today.
Unlike human names, unicorn names are gender-interchangeable.

Sparkle	Marshmallow	Buttercup	Starshine
Mystic	Rainbow	Eunice	Muffin
Whimsy	Sprinkle	Stabby	Twinkle

The unicorn then progresses
to a full-grownlcorn!

THE MANE EVENT: STYLING INSPIRATION FROM UNICORNS

Do unicorns ever style their manes?
The answer is: HECK YES!

With such lustrous manes and tails, how could they resist? While many unicorns favor a simple braid, Topsy Tail, or barrettes, others like tinting their manes different colors. Some unicorns are extremely bold with their styling, following the example of pop stars or fairy tale characters

UNICORN HAIR 101

What is the unicorn's natural mane and tail color? Unicorns are born with a light violet-colored mane and tail, but can easily become unicorns of a different color by wishing it so (yes, that's their method of hair dye).

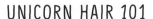

GETTING PRETTY:
HOW UNICORNS TREAT THEMSELVES

Curious about a unicorn's typical grooming routine? Hornicures
and hooficures are vital parts of the average unicorn spa day.

The average hornicure includes a soak, cleaning, buff, and,
if desired, polish. After the hornicure and hooficure, if a
unicorn is feeling particularly indulgent, he or she might also
opt for a little rump shiatsu or muzzle acupressure.

DO UNICORNS DATE?

1. Yes, unicorns date and even get married. Just like humans, many unicorns have a deep desire to find their forever partner. Also, they love wedding cake.

2. And yes, there are girl and boy unicorns; they often just have androgynously magical names that can make it hard to discern which is which.

3. They can make beautiful unicorn babies! We're not going to go into the details here, because, you know...privacy.

Just as on Earth, unicorns mostly start dating online. The most popular dating app in the Unicorniverse is *LuvBubble*, which allows unicorns to electronically transmit a bubble of magical intent and interest.

Once a unicorn finds his or her true love, it's for life. After all, if you found the perfect unicorn, wouldn't you hold on tight?

UNICORN Q+A
WITH SPRINKLE

When I met Sprinkle, I knew that we had a special connection, because the sparkles in our eyes matched. But it wasn't until one night, after a particularly raucous game of ring toss, that our conversations began to get serious. Over a gigantic plate of rainbow cookies, I really got to ask some hard-hitting questions, which I think you'll agree really reveal a lot about the unicorn's day-to-day life.

Are you real? If you believe in me, yes.

Is your blood really silver? I read that in Harry Potter. What monster would make a unicorn bleed? We tend to avoid that, and prefer to ooze magic.

What do you think of the unicorn food trend? FINALLY! All caps necessary.

What's your favorite food? If it is sweet and rainbow-colored, I'm in.

What's your last name? Cuddles. My full name is Sprinkle Sunshine Cuddles, the Third.

Do you have a job? Being mystical and magical 24/7?

Can I ride you? My goodness, we just met!

Can you grant me a wish? Maybe tomorrow.

How do you feel about humans? I love them just as much as they love me.

DONUT STOP BELIEVIN'

How long do unicorns live? The short answer is
unicorns will live as long as you believe in them.

Provided that unicorns eat well, enjoy plenty of magic,
and follow a strict regimen of fun and happiness,
it is possible for them to live forever.
What keeps them alive is how much we believe
in their magic, so never, ever,
EVER stop believing!

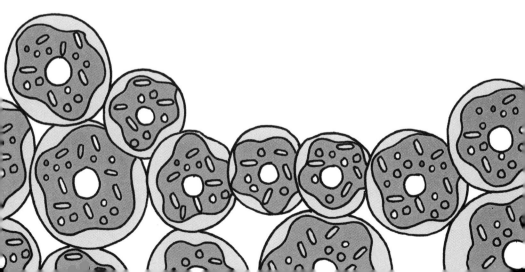

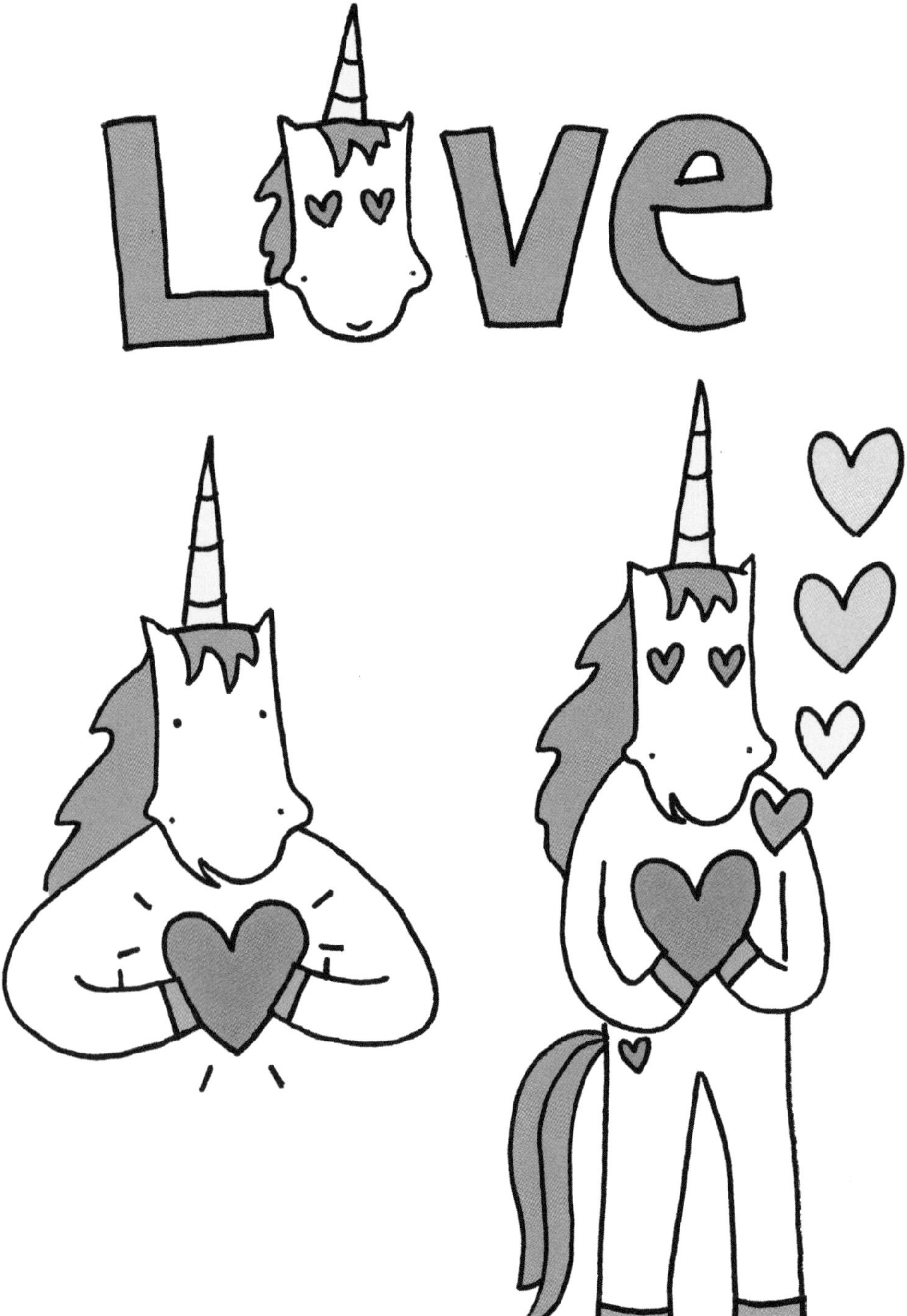
Love

Part 2

A UNICORN'S FAVORITE THINGS

Have you ever wondered what kind of stuff a unicorn really loves (and doesn't love) and why? You're in luck. In the next few pages, we'll explore all the things that make unicorns feel like their hearts and souls have been bedazzled with love and covered in pearlescent puffy paint, and all the other things that make them want to stamp their hooves in frustration.

COTTON CANDY

With the exception of a few buttercream cloud forests and a sprinkling of cumulus marshmallows, most of the clouds in the unicorn world are made of cotton candy. Cotton candy is great for prancing around on and snuggling up with at night, and is also considered a staple of the unicorn diet.

CUPCAKES

Did you know that in the Unicorniverse, there's a mandatory pleasure regimen? It's like their equivalent of the physical fitness test in elementary school, but far more enjoyable. One of the key ingredients in any routine of joy is cupcakes. They are sweet, they are delicious, and sharing is not necessary. Unicorns love 'em.

HEARTS AND STARS

Hearts and stars are super important in the Unicorniverse.
Love is everything to unicorns. In fact, over time unicorns
have even evolved to have a heart-shaped marking just
above the tail on their sweet little rumps.

Stars represent magic, and those shooting star sidekicks that
hang around unicorns are a constant reminder of this.

RAINBOWS...DUH!

Rainbows provide mental and physical nutrition for unicorns. Visually, the spectrum of all of the colors at once makes them happy and joyful. Eating rainbow-hued treats, such as cakes and donuts, or just about anything coated in rainbow sprinkles, makes their coats glisten and shine!

DONUTS

We already know that a unicorn's horn originally evolved as a donut-holding appendage, and while unicorns aren't necessarily transporting donuts on a daily basis these days, they still love those holey treats. The exception is cream-filled or jelly donuts. All unicorns agree that these treats are delicious, but they can't quite be stored in the same way...

GROSS.

RING TOSS

The unicorn's horn is perfect for ring toss. Unicorns typically play ring toss with donuts, though these days they usually use faux donuts to avoid getting icing on their horns and to discourage potential donut waste.

PRINCESSES

Unicorns love everything about princesses, including their daintiness, their decked-out enchanted castle homes, the soundtracks of the movies inspired by them, and the fact that tiny birds carry the trains of their dresses as they walk.

(GOOD) WITCHES

Good witches are valued allies of the unicorns. The relationship works favorably on both sides: witches can help cast a "bubble of positivity" spell for unicorns when visiting the human world, and unicorns can give witches a ride if their brooms break down.

Unicorns can quickly go incognito if they borrow a witch's hat.

BUTTERFLIES

Magical little wisps with brightly colored wings who fly around like little feather ballerinas? You bet your bottom donut that unicorns love butterflies.

BUTTERCREAM

Unicorns like to say that they love cake decorating, but let's be clear: more buttercream goes in their mouths than on top of any cake. Can you blame them?

FASHION MAGAZINES

They love a statement outfit and especially love the high fashion and couture magazines found at grocery store checkouts. They particularly love keeping tabs on Katy Perry's fabulous wardrobe.

BIRTHDAY PARTIES

Did you know that every single unicorn's birthday is treated as a national holiday in the Unicorniverse? This means their social calendars are always packed. Don't you think your life would be more magical if you got presents and ate birthday cake every day?

CARTWHEELS

You may think it's kind of cool to be suspended in the air with only
your horn making contact with the earth. But like the heel of a
stiletto pump, the unicorn's horn is somewhat unsteady, so unless
they have extremely good balance, they tend to avoid gymnastics.

SOCCER

While you may not necessarily describe unicorns as sporty, they do enjoy some physical activities. Soccer is not among those sports. All it takes is one header with a pointy horn and the soccer ball is toast.

(MOST) HATS

Fedoras, sunhats, and even baseball caps all suffer the same fate when you're a unicorn: horn blowout. However, unicorns are among the few living creatures who can actually pull off wearing visors without looking foolish. Party and princess hats also fit perfectly!

TEXTING

Texting, along with activities like handling a can opener and making cat's cradle formations with yarn, is not part of the unicorn's everyday life.

ROBOTS

The robot's rational nature and technical talk tend to grate on most unicorns. I mean, they communicate in zeros and ones! Just how much fun can they be anyway?

↑
AT
AN
impasse →

NEUTRALS AND EARTH TONES

You probably don't need a unicorn to tell you this, but neutrals and earth tones are totally boring. Why would you surround yourself with colors like taupe, khaki, and terra-cotta when you can have a rainbow instead?

I just don't get it.

Part 3

SEEKING UNICORNS

If deep in your cotton candy—loving heart you're hoping that someday, somehow, one way or another, you'll encounter a real live unicorn, but you aren't sure how to go about it, then this next section is for you. The following pages are designed to help you find unicorns in real life, with tips on understanding how unicorns think when visiting the human world, directions to top destinations for unicorn lovers, and the scoop on common unicorn hiding spots.

UNICORNS AREN'T AS HARD TO FIND AS YOU THINK

One of the first questions Sprinkle the unicorn gets asked by humans is: "Why are unicorns so hard to find?" Turns out, unicorns are not as rare as you think. The problem is that our human senses have become dulled to sighting unicorns. The more time you spend imagining, eating candy, and smiling, the more easily you'll be able to spot unicorns.

so busy

so importANt

Rare Unicorn Types

The following rare unicorn varieties are only seen once in a blue moonicorn, so if you should happen upon one, be sure to thank your lucky stars!

unicondor

Zebracorn

unicornish game hen

kangaroonicorn

ewenicorn

baboonicorn

I'M MOO-GICAL!

unicow

WON'T YOU TELL ME HOW TO GET TO...UNICORN STREET?

Want to go on a magical, mystical unicorn tour? Try visiting these spots all over the United States! (Warning: real unicorns may or may not be found.)

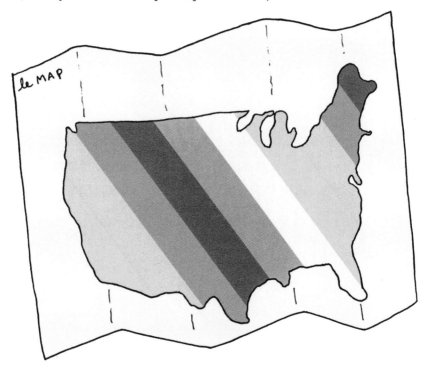

Unicorn Avenue, Madrid, IA

Unicorn Avenue, Port Richey, FL

Unicorn Circle, Amesbury, MA

Unicorn Circle, Ventura, CA

Unicorn Circle Northwest, Rio Rancho, NM

Unicorn Drive, Knoxville, TN

Unicorn Drive, Sanborn, NY

Unicorn Farm Road, Asheville, NC

Unicorn Lake Boulevard, Denton, TX (and yes, it is in fact right next to Unicorn Lake)

Unicorn Lane, Zirconia, NC

Unicorn Lane NW, Washington, DC

Unicorn Place, Capitol Heights, MD

Unicorn Place, Thomasville, NC

North Unicorn Street, Mead, WA

Unicorn Street, Las Vegas, NV

Unicorn Street, Monsey, NY

Unicorn Street, Newburyport, MA

Unicorn Street NW, Ramsey, MN

Unicorn Park Drive, Woburn, MA

Unicorn Way, Clifton, NJ

WHERE TO FIND UNICORNS: DESTINATIONS

Looking for a unicorn adventure?
The following locales are famous for their unicorn ties.

1. Lake Superior State University, Sault Ste. Marie, Michigan.

Talk about higher learning: since 1971, the university has been issuing Unicorn Questing licenses to a group called The Unicorn Hunters. Yikes! Don't worry, though; harming unicorns isn't the name of this hunting game. It's more a journey of self-discovery to embrace your uniqueness.

2. The HMS *Unicorn*, Dundee, Scotland.

Listed as part of the National Historic Fleet, the ship *Unicorn* is now a museum in Dundee, Scotland, United Kingdom.

HMS UNICORN*

* ACTUAL SHIP MAY VARY

3. Unicorn Cave, Germany.

Should you find yourself in the Harz Mountains, take the time to visit Unicorn Cave and pay your respects to past unicorns. It's said to be an ancient burial place for the horned creatures.

4. Unicorn Tapestries, New York City.

Nestled in the castle-like Cloisters museum, you'll find a series of intricate tapestries focused on capturing a unicorn. If you talk to any modern-day unicorn, he or she will tell you that there's no need to capture them. Just offer some bubble gum and Funfetti cupcakes and you've got a friend for life.

5. Unicorn, Seattle.

If you love creative food and drink, then be sure to check out Unicorn, a carnival-themed bar (and its sister location, Narwhal) in the hipster heaven that is Capitol Hill, Seattle. Ahem, uni-corndogs are on the menu.

6. Unicorn Cafe, Bangkok, Thailand.

This glitter-and-unicorn paraphernalia-packed cafe features magical, rainbow-colored cuisine. Be sure to look it up online—you won't regret it.

KEEP YOUR EYES PEELED!

Unicorns love to keep us humans on our toes. Here are just a few of the places you might come across a unicorn hanging out:

there's a horn under that cone!

Ice cream shops: Unicorns *love* ice cream...with rainbow sprinkles, of course. If you ever go to an ice cream shop and see a pony wearing an ice cream cone on its head, it's probably a unicorn. But shhh. Don't tell!

Party City, USA: Cities such as Las Vegas and New Orleans are great spots for unicorn sightings. The "anything goes" attitude and flashy fashion appeal to unicorns' love of glitter and color, and also allow them to move around incognito.

Princess parties: Par-tay! Princess parties have so much that unicorns love: princesses, crafts and games, birthday cake, and plenty of pink. Also, a princess hat fits perfectly over a unicorn's horn, making her invisible to partygoers.

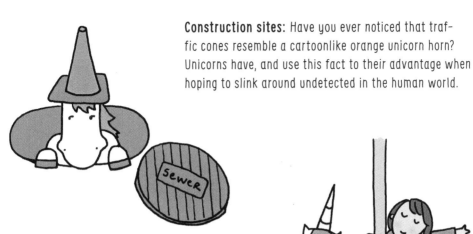

Construction sites: Have you ever noticed that traffic cones resemble a cartoonlike orange unicorn horn? Unicorns have, and use this fact to their advantage when hoping to slink around undetected in the human world.

Merry-go-rounds: Unicorns can frequently be found hiding in plain sight on merry-go-rounds (they love the music). It's possible that you or someone you know has ridden a unicorn and *didn't even know it.*

↑ ActuaL
UNICORN,
iNCogNito

COTTON CANDY!

Wherever cotton candy is sold: Cotton candy is to unicorns as catnip is to cats. Wherever cotton candy can be found, you can be pretty certain that there are unicorns somewhere close by. County fairs, baseball games, and carnivals are all common hangouts.

INTERSPECIES BFFS

Want to make friends with unicorns? Edge your way into their inner circle by making friends with their friends. Who are a unicorn's friends? Here are some of their beasties—er, besties:

Dragons: While unicorns tend to avoid fire-breathing dragons, they do love the sweet and kind ones who appear in folk songs.

Narwhals: After many years of strained relations (see note on next page), unicorns and narwhals have patched things up and are now the best of friends. Narwhals, also known as unicorns of the sea, love getting together with unicorns for hornicures and gossip.

Shooting stars: Catching a shooting star isn't easy, but if you do catch one and become its best friend, chances are pretty good that a unicorn friendship isn't far behind.

Adorable animals: Unicorns love cuddling with adorable animals, including, but not limited to, pug puppies, kittens, and baby bunnies. Awww!

 ← Food

 ← Friend

UNICORNS AND NARWHALS: THE UNTOLD STORY

Unicorns and narwhals have had a complex relationship over the years. There was even a several-hundred-year period when people were hunting narwhals and stealing their horns and then selling them as unicorn horns. As you might imagine, narwhals were pretty mad about this, and gave unicorns some epic silent treatment for a long time. Eventually unicorns and narwhals decided that it would be more productive to forge a friendship. Today, they are thick as thieves!

ATTRACTING UNICORNS

Dear humans: do you want to make yourself more desirable to potential unicorn friends? Here are some easy yet potentially life-transforming (for the better) tips for how to make yourself a true unicorn magnet:

Turn that frown upside down. Do you think that unicorns are going to be attracted to frowns, selfie pouts, or that terrible face you make while jogging? Not so much. Bright and happy smiles and a sunny disposition are much better choices.

Employ unicorn keywords. Try using unicorn keywords, such as "magic," "rainbow," "mystical," and "sparklelicious," in casual conversation. You may be surprised to see how natural it feels after only a short time.

When in doubt, add rainbow sprinkles and/or glitter. After the age of six or so, humans tend to become much more cautious with their use of both rainbow sprinkles and glitter. Reverse the curse and begin using these magical substances whenever you can!

Cuddle more. Unicorns take notice when they see proactive and enthusiastic cuddlers. Just think—one day you could be cuddling with a unicorn.

Throw out all of the black, gray, brown, and beige in your closet. These colors are largely considered boring by unicorns. Gray shoes are an exception, as they match a unicorn's hooves.

Outfit your desk with Lisa Frank accessories. Break out your Trapper Keeper and Lisa Frank–brand desk accessories, and make sure they are front and center on your work surface.

Prominently display any unicorn-related decor. If you have any unicorn figurines, statuettes, pillows, or other decorations, be sure to display them proudly in your home. Some avid unicorn-seekers have even doctored reindeer lawn ornaments to resemble unicorns.

Plant donut seeds in your front yard. How else will you grow a unicorn-attracting donut tree?

UNICORN DOS AND DON'TS

Do compliment a unicorn on his or her lustrous mane.

Don't comment on the size of a unicorn's horn.

Do ask a unicorn about his or her opinion on cupcakes.

Don't tell a unicorn about your juice fast.

Do ask a unicorn for a hug.

Don't ask if a unicorn is, in fact, the last unicorn.

Do offer a unicorn a bite (better yet, half) of your Pop-Tart.

Don't tell a unicorn you prefer cake without frosting.

Do show a unicorn your Lisa Frank sticker collection.

Don't try to hang your handbag from a unicorn's horn. Rude.

Do ask a unicorn for fashion advice.

Don't ever call a unicorn "imaginary" or "a fantasy."

Do suggest a game of ring toss.

Don't ask to play leap frog. Ever.

Unicorn-y jokes

Unicorns love jokes. The cornier, the better! Practice with a few of these and you'll have an eager unicorn audience in no time.

What do you call a unicorn on Spring Break? A Cancúnicorn.

What might you call a unicorn that hails from Hawaii's capital? A Honolulucorn (try saying that five times fast!).

What does a unicorn ballerina wear?
A tutunicorn.

What kind of unicorn can you wear
on your foot? A shoenicorn.

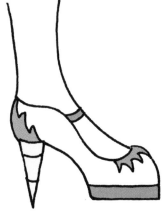

What do you call a cross between a unicorn and a cream puff? A choux-nicorn.

How do unicorns prefer their ice cream? In a unicone.

What do you call a unicorn who loves to knit? A yarnicorn.

What do unicorns put on their Christmas trees? Unicornaments.

What does a unicorn say when it sneezes? Achoonicorn (don't forget to be polite and say "bless younicorn" after!).

What's the biggest attraction at Unicorn Se World? Shamunicorn.

What do you say to a unicorn who is just about to depart on a big trip? Adieunicorn (also acceptable: "see you soonicorn").

the Unicorn food pyramid

Part 4

WWUE?
(WHAT WOULD
UNICORNS EAT?)

While it's important for humans to eat a
good balance of protein, carbohydrates,
healthy fats, and other boring stuff, unicorns
have different health requirements. Cotton
candy is the name of the game here, along
with cake, ice cream, and a slice of pizza or
a fruit- or vegetable-based sweet every now
and again. In the following pages, you'll find
a synopsis of unicorn food culture as well
as some unicorn-approved recipes to try
at home!

UNICORN FOOD TREND

Food! Glorious unicorn food! For the past few years, unicorns have been making a big splash in the culinary arena. What started with rainbow cake and "unicorn poop" cookies has expanded into a worldwide phenomenon, with unicorn-themed dishes of every sort, from ice cream sundaes and pancakes to bagels and...yes, even sushi.

The following so-called unicorn foods are inspired by unicorns, but designed for human consumption. What makes a dish unicorn-worthy can vary: it may be literally decorated like a unicorn, or it could simply be a version of a food that features rainbow coloring, rainbow sprinkles, and plenty of sparkle. If you are what you eat, be magical and sweet!

UNICORN TOAST

Makes 1 serving

INGREDIENTS:

1 slice toast

1–2 tablespoons soft cream cheese

Food coloring in red, orange, yellow, green, blue, and violet

Sprinkles (optional)

1. Place the toast on a plate. Spread the cream cheese on the top third of the slice (it will be thick).

2. Starting on one side, apply a dot of each color of food coloring on the cream cheese.

3. Use a butter knife to spread the cream cheese across the other two-thirds of the slice of toast, dragging the food coloring as you spread. Clean the knife after spreading each color, so that you don't end up with unintended or unattractive color-mixing.

4. If desired, add sprinkles. Enjoy immediately.

RAINBOW SUGAR CUBES

Sugar cubes are an ideal starting place if you want to eat, drink, and think like a unicorn. By tinting them multiple colors, you'll make them more magical. You can snack on them alone or stir them into your next unicorn latte.

Prep time: 10 minutes active time, plus several hours to harden

Yields approximately 24 (1 teaspoon-sized) portions

INGREDIENTS:

½ cup granulated sugar

1 teaspoon water

Food coloring in as many colors as you'd like

A small silicone candy mold with small vessels (can be cubes or another shape of your liking)

Note: Silicone candy molds with fairly small individual holes are ideal for this project. Their flexible material allows the cubes to be extracted easily and gives a smooth, even finish. However, plastic molds or even an ice cube tray with small holes can also be used.

1. Pour sugar into a large mixing bowl. Add water and then mix with a fork until it is moistened; it will have a texture like brown sugar.

2. Divide the mixture into as many separate bowls as you have colors. Add a drop or two of food coloring into each bowl, and mix up your respective colors.

3. Using a spoon, transfer about 1 teaspoon of the sugar into each hole of your mold (it can be all one color or a little bit of a few colors). Pack the sugar very firmly, as you really want it to press into the shape of the mold.

4. Let the cubes sit at room temperature for several hours or overnight so they can harden. If you choose to cover them, do so loosely.

5. Extract the molded sugar cubes from the mold. They should come out quite easily.

6. Store your finished sugar cubes in a breathable container (such as a paper bag or a covered sugar dish). These will keep for several months.

RAINBOW SPRINKLE MARSHMALLOWS

Did you know that "Marshmallow" is one of the most common names for unicorns? It's about as common as the name "Steve" in the human world. Marshmallows are also an important part of any unicorn's diet. These perfectly sweet pillows of marshmallowy bliss can be rainbow-fied with rainbow sprinkles!

Note: This recipe can be made with honey or light corn syrup if you don't have or don't like the flavor of maple syrup. If using corn syrup, it's suggested that you add 1–2 teaspoons of vanilla extract for added flavor.

Prep time: 30 minutes active time, plus about 3 hours to set

Yields about 32 jumbo marshmallows

INGREDIENTS:

1 cup room-temperature water, divided

3 envelopes unflavored gelatin

2 cups granulated sugar

½ cup maple syrup

½ teaspoon salt

1 cup rainbow sprinkles

About 2 cups confectioners' sugar

1. Generously grease an 8" square baking pan and one side of a sheet of parchment paper that's slightly larger than the pan (but don't put the parchment paper in the pan). Set aside.

2. Pour ½ cup of the water into the bowl of a stand mixer. Sprinkle the gelatin as evenly as you can on top. Fit the mixer with the whisk attachment.

3. Combine the remaining water, sugar, maple syrup, and salt in a medium saucepan. Heat on medium-high, stirring frequently. Let the mixture come to a boil for 1 minute, and then remove from heat.

4. Go back to your mixer! Turn the mixer on low and mix the now-thick water and gelatin mixture until combined. With the mixer still on low, carefully pour in the hot sugar mixture. Be careful and go slow so as not to spatter.

5. Once the mixture is combined, increase the mixing speed to high. Mix for 10 minutes, or until the mixture is thickened and at least doubled in size. When the mixture looks ready, add the vanilla (if using) and rainbow sprinkles, and mix just briefly to incorporate.

continued on next page >>>

6. Now it's time to work quickly, as the mixture will set rapidly and become hard to handle once you stop mixing. Spread the thick, sticky mixture into your prepared baking pan. It will be quite full, about flush with the rim of the pan (don't overfill).

7. Press the parchment paper, greased side down, on top of the mixture and smooth with your hands to flatten the tops of the marshmallows.

8. Now it's time to wait. Let the marshmallows set (with the parchment still on top) for at least 3 hours for an optimal texture.

9. Generously dust a work surface with confectioners' sugar. Use a knife to loosen the edges of your marshmallows, then invert the pan onto the sugar. Dust more sugar on top.

10. Cut the marshmallows out! Cut into large rectangles of about 2" x 1" wide (which will give you four rows of eight jumbo 'mallows). Alternately, you can use cookie cutters or a knife to cut them into whatever sizes and shapes you like. Be sure to dust the cutter/knife and the sides of the cut marshmallows with confectioners' sugar.

11. Store in an airtight container with layers divided by parchment paper. These marshmallows will keep for up to 2 weeks.

SOMEWHERE OVER THE RAINBOW SUGAR COOKIES

Picture this: you're on your first friend-date with a unicorn, and you really want to make a good impression. If you have these cookies to offer as a snack, you'll be upgrading to best friend necklace territory in no time. Easy to make with minimal ingredients, these vibrant rainbow sugar cookies are as dazzling as they are delicious.

Prep time: 2 hours, 15 minutes (includes chilling time for dough)

Bake time: 7–9 minutes

Yields about 60 small (approximately 1½") cookies

INGREDIENTS:

2¼ cups all-purpose flour

½ teaspoon salt

2 sticks unsalted butter, softened

1 cup confectioners' sugar, sifted

1 teaspoon vanilla extract

Food coloring in red, orange, yellow, green, blue, and violet

1. In a medium bowl, sift together the flour and salt. Set aside.

2. Cream the butter in the bowl of a stand mixer fitted with the paddle attachment for 2–3 minutes on medium speed, or until nice and fluffy. Add the confectioners' sugar and mix on medium-low speed until all of the sugar has been absorbed. Stir in the vanilla.

3. Add the flour mixture in 2 or 3 increments, mixing on low speed. Use a rubber spatula to scrape down the bowl as needed. The dough will be very soft.

4. Divide the dough into 6 equal portions. Tint each portion with your respective colors. Go vibrant, because food coloring fades a little bit in the oven. If you don't relish wearing rainbows on your hands, wear gloves for this part.

5. Divide each tinted portion into four equal parts (so you'll have 24 portions of dough, 4 portions each of 6 different colors). Roll each portion into a thin, slender snake, about 6" long.

continued on next page >>>

6. Assemble your rainbows! Grab one tube of each color of dough, and press them all together to form a new, larger tube. Press the dough portions together firmly, to ensure that the colors stay together. Roll into a new log, pressing and compressing the dough, and then roll it into a new, approximately 8" long log. Repeat the process with the remaining portions, so that you'll now end up with four tubes of rainbow dough.

7. Wrap each portion securely with plastic wrap and place in the refrigerator for at least 2 hours to chill (overnight is fine).

8. Near the end of your chilling time, line two baking sheets with parchment paper and preheat the oven to 375°F. Remove the dough from the fridge and let it soften slightly.

9. Cut the dough into approximately ½"-thick slices (you'll get about 15 slices per portion of dough). If the dough is too tough to work with, let it soften another minute or two before proceeding.

10. Place the dough portions on the prepared baking sheets. They can be fairly close together, as these cookies don't spread too much, so you should be able to fit 30 per sheet.

11. Bake for 7–9 minutes, or until the cookies have a matte finish on top and slight browning on the sides and bottom. Remove from the oven; let the cookies cool on the pans for several minutes before transferring to a wire rack to cool completely.

12. Store these cookies in an airtight container at room temperature for up to one week or freeze for up to one month.

FOODS UNICORNS DON'T LOVE

Cookies with Raisins

Talk about creating trust issues... Similar to many humans, unicorns are deeply traumatized when they bite into a cookie only to find that what they thought were delicious chocolate chips are actually disappointing raisins.

"Why would anyone do that?" they implore.

Unicorns, we feel your pain.

Chocolate Sprinkles

Unicorns love chocolate *and* they love sprinkles. But let's face it: chocolate sprinkles are kind of ugly. In a world where rainbow sprinkles exist, unicorns really have no idea why anyone would ever choose such an unattractive option as the chocolate sprinkles.

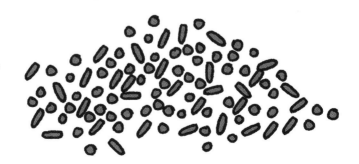

EDIBLE GLITTER

Make everything that you eat shimmer (literally) with edible glitter! This easy-to-make recipe allows you to transform gelatin, water, and food coloring into a sparkling food glaze. It requires a little time to "set," so be sure to get to work a day before you want to garnish your cookies, cake, or pizza (what?).

Prep time: 20 minutes active time, plus several hours to harden

Yields 2–3 tablespoons of glitter (it may sound like a little, but glitter-wise, that's quite a lot)

INGREDIENTS:

4 tablespoons water, divided

1 envelope unflavored gelatin

Pearlescent powder or pearlescent gel food coloring

SPECIAL SUPPLIES:

A nonstick work surface (a silicone liner works best, though parchment paper is okay)

1. Prepare your work surface by setting your silicone liner inside of a rimmed baking sheet.

2. Pour 1 tablespoon of cold water into a medium bowl. Sprinkle the gelatin evenly on top. Use a small whisk to mix the water and gelatin (it may look a little lumpy, but don't worry).

3. Heat the remaining 3 tablespoons of water in a saucepan until boiling. Since it's a small amount of water, you may find this is easiest to do in a heatproof cup in the microwave, heating the water in 20-second blasts on high until it begins to bubble.

4. Carefully pour the hot water on top of the cold water/gelatin and whisk to combine. Once the gelatin is dissolved, stir in your pearlescent coloring, and keep whisking until evenly dispersed.

5. Let the mixture set until it begins to thicken to the point where you can lift the whisk and the mixture drips from the whisk very slowly.

6. Using either a pastry brush or a spatula, spread the sparkly gelatin mixture onto your work surface. If it begins to form beads and doesn't spread well, wait 1 minute before proceeding. At the right time, it will stay put in a thin layer with minimal holes. But don't worry too much if it's not 100 percent even, or if it has small bubbles. You will be grinding it into glitter later on anyway.

7. Wait for the sheet of gelatin to harden. You want a hard, brittle form. It can take some time, so allow for several hours or even overnight, depending on the humidity of your kitchen.

8. Cut the sheets into small shards using kitchen scissors (this will make it easier to grind). Place these shards into a blender, and grind into a fine powder. Store in an empty spice jar. This glitter will keep for up to 6 months. Put it on everything!

THE TRUE STORY OF CUPCAKES

Are you curious about how cupcakes were *really* invented?
Here's the true story, as told by unicorns.

and on that ride...

UNICORN DONUTS

Donut worry, eat happy! This recipe allows you to celebrate unicorns and one of their favorite foods. Decorate your donuts like unicorns with this easy tutorial!

Prep time: 30 minutes

Yields 6 donuts

INGREDIENTS:

6 plain donuts

½ cup shredded coconut

Red, blue, and yellow food coloring

6 ounces white chocolate chips

¼ cup whole milk

¾ cup confectioners' sugar

6 pieces candy corn

Rainbow sprinkles

Black writing icing

1. Grab your wire rack and set it up over a sheet of parchment paper to catch drips. Have your donuts ready and set to the side.

2. Tint your coconut by putting it in a plastic sandwich bag, adding a couple of drops each of red and blue coloring, and shaking it until it's nice and violet.

3. Make the glaze. In the top of a double boiler, combine the white chocolate chips and milk. Heat over medium-low heat until the chips have mostly melted. Remove from heat and stir. Any solid bits should melt in the residual heat. Let it sit until slightly thickened, then whisk in the confectioners' sugar. The mixture should be thick and mostly opaque.

4. Reserve a small portion of the glaze (about ¼ cup) in a separate, small bowl. Add a couple of drops of yellow food coloring, and stir to combine.

5. Make the horns. Spear each piece of candy corn on a toothpick and dip it in the yellow mixture until fully coated (it may require 2–3 dippings, letting it set in between). Let the horns set. You can do this by spearing the toothpicks in an extra donut, if you have one. If not, you can place them on a sheet of parchment paper.

continued on next page >>>

6. Back to the donuts and glaze! Dip the donuts in the glaze, one by one, turning to ensure even coverage. If the glaze seems too thin, let it thicken a few more minutes before proceeding. Remove and transfer to the wire rack so that they can set. If you see any spots that don't look fully covered, wait a few minutes and spoon some more of the glaze on top.

7. While the glaze is still slightly wet, start some decoration. On the back half of the freshly glazed donut, scatter a few rainbow sprinkles—this will help make your donuts festive.

8. Decide where you'll put the horn (the front top of the donut works well), and very delicately sprinkle a small amount of the coconut mixture on that spot. Be sure to leave enough room to put a face below it.

DONUT
WORRY,
BE HAPPY

9. Once the horns have set, remove from the toothpicks and press on top of the coconut tuft, pressing to form a seal. You may need to slightly move some of the coconut to the side or use a little leftover glaze to help it stick. If needed, apply a little more of that coconut mixture to cover up any messy edges.

10. Wait for the glaze to set. Finally, use your black writing icing, draw two downward facing curved lines to create delicately closed eyes, with a few eyelashes facing downward to indicate how sweet and dainty your unicorn is. Below that, add two simple dots for unicorn nostrils.

11. Store at room temperature in a single layer, well wrapped, for up to 2 days.

Part 5

HOW TO UNICORN-IFY YOUR LIFE

By now you should be fairly well versed in the ways of unicorns! It's time to take the next step and make your life a unicornucopia of magic. This section is action-packed with activities, tips, tricks, and resources to help unicorn-ify your life.

ADOPT THE UNICORN MINDSET

If you really want to unicorn-ify your life, the first step is to channel your inner unicorn. All it takes is asking yourself one simple question: what would a unicorn do?

It applies to every situation. Should you call your mom? Would you like to see the dessert menu? Is it a good day to take off from work and go get a massage and buy new shoes instead? In your heart, you know what a unicorn would choose.

EMBRACE '80S MOVIES AND '90S TV

One of the easiest ways to unicorn-ify your life is to embrace the '80s and '90s with all your heart! To put it simply: unicorns are obsessed with the many TV and movie staples that came out during these dazzling decades.

'80s Movies

It would be difficult to overstate how much unicorns truly love '80s movies. With their epic montages, incredible fashion, and upbeat soundtracks, they never fail to put unicorns in a great mood.

'90s TV

While unicorns adore the films of the '80s, they universally agree that '90s TV is where it's at. From *Clarissa Explains It All* to *The Adventures of Pete and Pete* (don't even get a unicorn started on *Saved by the Bell*), unicorns believe that the '90s were the true golden age of television.

UNICORN NAME GENERATOR

Fitting in with your new unicorn friends is far easier if you have an official unicorn name. Out of ideas? No problem. Use this quick and easy unicorn name generator to come up with an A+ nickname.

STEP 1: PICK YOUR BIRTH MONTH

JANUARY	FEBRUARY	MARCH	APRIL
Glitter	Confetti	Magic	Dainty

MAY	JUNE	JULY	AUGUST
Mystic	Darling	Rainbow	Sweetie

SEPTEMBER	OCTOBER	NOVEMBER	DECEMBER
Precious	Tender Loving	Sparkle	Enchanting

STEP 2: PICK YOUR BIRTH DATE

1.	2.	3.	4.
Bonbon	Pancake	Milkshake	Cuddles
5.	6.	7.	8.
Sprinkle	Buttercup	Cookie	Gumdrop
9.	10.	11.	12.
Cream Puff	Kisses	Bunny	Giggles
13.	14.	15.	16.
Cupcake	Bubblegum	Sugarcube	Moonbeam
17.	18.	19.	20.
Starshine	Pompom	Moon Pie	Muffin
21.	22.	23.	24.
Blossom	Snickerdoodle	Marshmallow	Sunbeam
25.	26.	27.	28.
Snowflake	Munchkin	Sunshine	Bubbles
29.	30.	31.	
Cotton Candy	Dumpling	Nugget	

Dang! That's a great unicorn name!

HOW TO HOST A UNICORN PARTY

Unicorns are always looking for an opportunity to party. Birthdays are a big deal, of course, but even something as simple as buying a new tub of rainbow sprinkles can inspire a celebration. Luckily, in the human world, you can party like a unicorn on your birthday or any day by following these tips.

Attire: Be sure to specify that a unicorn horn is mandatory. Alternately, you can provide a station with materials for making a horn.

Drinks: Have something festive like champagne or pink lemonade to serve too. Garnish your cocktails/mocktails with cotton candy. Yummy!

Music: Craft a mystical playlist!

Greeting: Upon entering the party, assign everyone a unicorn name. Use the handy unicorn name generator for help!

Food: As for cuisine, you could go in a few different directions or a combination of the three:

- Sweets (perhaps some from this book!)
- Rainbow foods (sweet or savory)
- Foods that incorporate "unicorn" in the title (ex: uni-corndogs, uni-cornbread, choux-nicorn pastries, etc.)

Decor: Twinkle lights, crepe paper, and everything sparkly and bright. Glitter is highly encouraged. While unicorns don't advocate violence, they love piñatas, particularly if filled with rainbow candy.

Activities: There are plenty of activities to choose from in this section of the book. Additionally, pin the horn on the unicorn and unicorn horn ring toss are always great ideas.

UNICORN PLAYLIST

Dance like a unicorn! Play these songs at your next unicorn party and everyone's hooves will be in the air like they just don't care.

"I Want Candy" by Bow Wow Wow

"Do You Believe in Magic?" by the Lovin' Spoonful

"Sugar Sugar" by the Archies

"Tutti Frutti" by Little Richard

"Sunshine, Lollipops, and Rainbows" by Lesley Gore

"Good Day Sunshine" by the Beatles

"Fantasy" by Mariah Carey

"Cotton Candy Land" by Elvis Presley

"Daydream Believer" by the Monkees

"MMMBop" by Hanson

"Lollipop" by the Chordettes

"Candy" by Iggy Pop

"She's a Rainbow" by the Rolling Stones

"Puff, the Magic Dragon" by Peter, Paul & Mary

"Who Loves the Sun?" by the Velvet Underground

"Heaven Is a Place on Earth" by Belinda Carlisle

"Barbie Girl" by Aqua

SOUNDTRACK FUN!

Soundtracks such as *The Wizard of Oz*, *Dirty Dancing*, and any princess movie you can think of are all great music choices for unicorn parties.

UNICORNS IN FILM

Sometimes you just feel like kicking back and enjoying a UNI (Unicorn's Night In). Next time you're having the urge to cozy up and watch some unicorn-centric cinema, check out one of these films. Can you spy a unicorn in all of them?

Blade Runner (yes, really)

Fantasia (both the old and new ones)

Harold & Kumar Go to White Castle

Harry Potter and the Sorcerer's Stone (released as *Harry Potter and the Philosopher's Stone* in some countries)

The Last Unicorn

Legend

The Chronicles of Narnia: The Lion, the Witch, and the Wardrobe

Nico the Unicorn

The Secret of Moonacre

Unico

HOW TO MAKE A UNICORN HORN

Talk to any unicorn and he or she will tell you that life will be more unicorn-ful if you make yourself (and your friends) some DIY unicorn horns. This tutorial is easy to follow, requires minimal supplies, and can easily be adapted using whatever supplies or glitter you have on hand.

Makes 1 horn

SUPPLIES:

1 (9" x 12") sheet of adhesive glitter foam

Scissors

A glue gun

1 plastic headband

Sequins, glitter, ribbon, or other flair of your choosing

1. Turn your foam sheet horizontally so that it is 12" wide and 9" tall. Cut it in half so that you have two 6" x 9" portions. You'll only need one, so you can use the remaining sheet for decorations.

2. Remove the adhesive and roll into a horn shape by starting on one of the short sides and rolling it inward (give it a practice round or two with the adhesive on if that seems confusing at first).

3. Trim the bottom of the horn shape so that it is flat.

4. Hold your horn against the top of your headband, and determine which parts of the horn will require glue to stick. Using a glue gun, apply glue to the horn and affix it to your headband. If desired, you can cut a square from the remaining glitter adhesive paper that is slightly larger than the base of the horn and affix it, facing up, below the headband, to help keep the horn secure.

5. Decorate! Use your glue gun to stick sequins, glitter, ribbon, or any other awesome added detailing. Be sure to let the glue dry before you wear your unicorn horn!

MAKE YOUR OWN UNICORN STORY

Build your very own unicorn story with this unicorn Mad Libs! You can make it a group effort at your next unicorn party or give it a try by yourself. Both are unicorn approved.

Name a:

1. Plural noun
2. Girl unicorn name
3. Adjective
4. Pop song
5. Article of clothing
6. Hairstyle
7. Same unicorn's name
8. Plural creature
9. Exclamation!
10. Adjective
11. Number
12. Noun
13. Boy unicorn name
14. Emotion
15. Favorite game
16. Time of day
17. Plural noun
18. Adjective
19. Adjective
20. Emotion

The Unicorn Party

My oh my, was it an extra-special with (1)-on-top day for (2) the unicorn. It was her birthday, and she was looking (3). She was getting ready for the party in her room, singing (4) while putting on her favorite (5). Her best friend was helping to style her mane in a (6).

Party time! When (7) walked into the room, there was a large crowd of (8) waiting to yell "(9)!" and greet her with a (10) pile of (11) presents. Her favorite gift was a (12) from her secret crush, (13). She felt so (14).

After opening presents and playing several rounds of (15), they danced and pranced until (16). Then it was time for cake! The cake was festooned with (17) and looked absolutely (18).

This was absolutely the (19) birthday ever, and she told everyone, "I feel so (20)!"

127

HOW TO WRITE LETTERS LIKE A UNICORN

Unicorns have a unique way of writing letters: they whisper messages into rainbow rays, and then they wish them over to their friends, who are greeted with not only a rainbow but good tidings as well.

Sadly, humans do not have the magic ability to do this.

But we can snag the idea and send a friend a bouquet of rainbows and sweetness by stuffing balloons with little notes and gifts. It basically guarantees a magical day for the recipient. Here's how to do it!

SUPPLIES:

Messages or small gifts to put in the balloons

A variety of rainbow-colored balloons

A shipping box

Tissue paper and packing material

Love

1. Start by preparing a bunch of small notes. You can also grab some other things, like candy or marbles, that will make nice little gifts for your friends.

2. Place the notes or gifts in the balloons. Try to keep it to one or two things per balloon. Roll up notes to get them inside of the balloons with ease.

3. Blow up the balloons. It is best to blow them up kind of small, about the size of a large apple.

4. Once you have a few balloons assembled, place them in a box lined with tissue paper. Line the sides and top with packing material before sealing and addressing the box.

5. Send it on its way! Unlike unicorns, you can't wish your package to its recipient, so you'll have go USPS, UPS, or FedEx. For best results, use a fairly rapid shipping method (such as priority mailing); otherwise, the balloons may deflate. Sad face!

HOW TO DRAW A UNICORN IN 8 EASY STEPS

Follow this simple tutorial to learn how to draw cartoonicorns and then cover every surface possible with your doodles!

1. Draw an arc with two pointing, upside-down, V-shaped protrusions (think delicate cat ears) on either side.

2. Lengthen the face by drawing straight lines extending below the ears.

3. Create the muzzle by drawing a downward-facing arc with a little bump on either side.

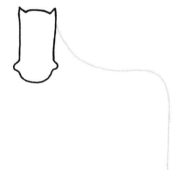

4. It's getting real now. Starting from just below one of the ears, draw a curving line that settles into a straight line; that will be the back of the hind leg of the unicorn. You can make it straight or angle the line this way or that.

5. Create the rest of the unicorn body by drawing three arcs punctuated with flat lines in between. Finish the body by drawing a line to connect the front leg with the face, and add little lines to form the hooves.

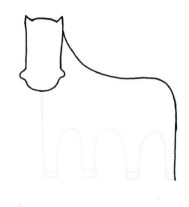

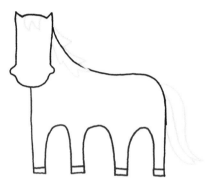

6. Add a mane and tail. If applicable, erase the line of the unicorn's body that might be under its lush mane.

7. Add the final details: two prominent dots for eyes, two smaller dots for nostrils, a heart near the unicorn's rump (optional but suggested), and, of course, the horn!

8. If desired, color your unicorn in, and be sure to give it a name. Say hello to your new friend!

SPOT THE DIFFERENCES!

Well, hello, glittering gumshoes!
Can you detect the 10 differences
between these two unicorn scenes?

Answers: 1. Top unicorn arm position | **2.** Different amount of ice cream scoops | **3.** Rainbow in opposite color order on bottom star | **4.** Face on pink heart in the center | **5.** Color of the rump heart | **6.** Sprinkles on lower right cupcake | **7.** Bottom cloud color | **8.** Color of hearts next to the ice cream unicorn | **9.** Front of mane on lower unicorn | **10.** Diamond ring is only in one image

UNICORN WISDOM FOR THE ROAD

Before these unicorns hit the road, they want to leave us humans with some parting words of wisdom. So go forth, magical humans, and be bright, be bold, be younicorn.

1. Lead with your heart, not your horn.

2. Be younicorn. Everybody else is already taken.

3. Spread happiness, delight, and rainbow glitter wherever you go.

4. Donut worry, be happy.

5. Believe in magic.

6. Be the unicorn you wish to see in the world.

7. If you are what you eat, be sweet.

8. When in doubt, add rainbow sprinkles.

9. Always order dessert.

10. Donut stop believin'.

Appendix

UNICORN PROFILES

Just as there are celebrities in the human world, there are unicorn celebrities in the Unicorniverse. Here are just a few of the most famous unicorns to date.

CREAM PUFF, PRIZE-WINNING PASTRY CHEF

Born near the sparkling seas of Buttercream Bay, Cream Puff took an interest in the culinary arts at an early age. While her early efforts weren't always particularly edible (rainbow macaroni and cheese cookies didn't work out quite the way she wanted), her parents were supportive of her interest, and eventually she honed her art at the prestigious Unicordon Bleu cooking academy.

Cream Puff decided to focus her fantastical efforts on pastries and sweets, and was quickly appointed the pastry chef at the unicorn institution Chateau Cotton Candy. Her famous cotton candy soufflé, precious pastries, and luscious layer cakes earned her the nicknames Maestro of Magic and Siren of Sugar.

Proudest achievement? When Narwhal Stewart (a domestic goddess and TV personality in the mystical world) declared my cotton candy soufflé "the most toothsome thing I've ever tasted."

What was your childhood nickname? Puff Mama.

What's your guilty pleasure? A glass of Unicôtes du Rhône and a toaster pastry after work.

What celebrity was nicest to you? Unicolonel Sanders.

Notable quotable: "When in doubt, add rainbow sprinkles."

GWENDOLYN SPARKLE, LIFESTYLE GURU

While Gwendolyn Sparkle famously said that she's "totally normal," others argued that she's had an extra-charmed life. Born to successful thespian unicorn parents, Gwendolyn pursued a film career in young adulthood, and even won a Sparkly for her performance in the Shakespearean comedy *Much Ado about Muffin*.

In recent years, she's perhaps better known as the founder of POUF, a unicorn lifestyle website known for its arguably over-the-top health tonics and product suggestions.

Proudest achievement? My two babycorns, Mossy and Chiclet.

Favorite snack? Rainbow juice.

Favorite book? The ones I've written, of course.

What's your beauty routine? An organic hornicure and mane blowout each day.

Notable quotable: "I'm incredibly close to the common unicorn."

CASSIUS CORN, ATHLETIC ALL-STAR

Cassius Corn is perhaps the most beloved unicorn sports hero of all time. His speed and natural grace were evident from an early age. He actually began his career as a dancer, but when he entered Unicorniversity, he discovered his true calling: ring toss.

Dubbed "the ring-dinger," Cassius has a unique approach to ring toss: freestyling with dance-like movements and whimsical bits of spoken-word poetry as he catches nearly every donut flung his way.

Proudest achievement? Breaking the World Ring Toss record at last year's DonutFest.

What's your guilty pleasure? Eating cream- or jelly-filled donuts (which are strictly forbidden on the actual ring toss field).

What's your go-to karaoke song? "Genie in a Bottle" by Christina Aguilera.

What's your post-workout snack?
A rainbow-chip smoothie.

Notable quotable:
"If at first you donut succeed, fry, fry again."

TAYLOR MIST, POP STAR

Over the past few years, Taylor Mist has successfully transitioned from preteen performer to reigning Top 40 pop star as a young ladycorn. With such hits as "Bake 'em Up" and "33," she is known for her energetic music videos, vibrant performances, and penchant for writing love songs about unicorn ex-suitors.

While she hasn't found her forever partner yet, she's having fun playing the field and gathering inspiration for future hit singles.

Proudest achievement?
Winning the Sequin Award for my album!

Favorite movie? Definitely *Dirty Prancing*.
"Nobody Puts Baby in the Unicorner!"

How do you unwind?
Gazing at a nice sunset, while
wearing a pretty dress.

What foods are always in your pantry?
Cotton candy. Duh!

Notable quotable: "I keep seeking
Prince Charming, but end up
only with toads."

SEAN UNI-CONNERY, UNICORN ACTOR

Hailing from a super secluded part of the unicorn world just above Scotland (where the unicorn is the national animal, BTW), Sean Uni-Connery emerged on the film scene with the breakout role of *James Wand*, a debonair wizard-spy unicorn.

With his signature brogue and quick wit, he quickly became a beloved actor who has enjoyed a long, storied career. For his fine work in *The Unicorntouchables*, he was awarded the Sparkly, the highest award in unicorn acting.

Proudest achievement?
I realized I'd made it when I was spoofed on a famous Saturday night comedy show.

What's your superpower?
My accent and the fact that I'm a unicorn.

What was the most fun movie to work on?
The League of Extraordinary Unicorns; the ensemble cast was an inspiration.

Notable quotable:
"Movies are just pretend, but unicorns are for real."